Walter
the
Wily Walleye

Walter says,

"GO Fishing for FUN!"

by
BOB ALLEN

Bob Allen

illustrated by
SCOTT ALBERTS

To my best catch, Annie. My love of fishing is only exceeded
by the love for my soulmate. She has respected my time on
the water and tolerated my passion for fishing.

To Chris and Nat, the finest sons a fisherman could hope for.
And to Parker, Julian and Blaze, grandsons that show promise to
carry on a love of life and appreciation for the outdoors.

— BA

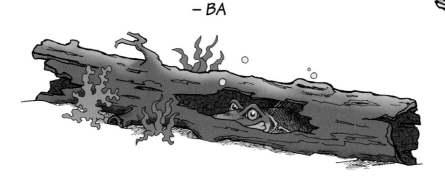

To Lynn, for allowing me to stay home and draw fishies and
cartoons rather than making me get a real job. Your love and
encouragement are more than I deserve.

And to our son Eric, for still including your Dad in so many
outdoor adventures. "Let's see where this trail goes…."

— SA

ISBN: 978-0-692-10292-3

Printed by Worzalla, Stevens Point, WI

Third Printing 2020

Illustrations, cover, and interior design by Scott Alberts

Fishing Quest Publishing
185 Leanore Lane
Brookfield, WI 53005

To order, visit www.boballenauthor.com · Call 262-844-5525 for reseller discounts.

to find midnight minnows
in shallows near the park.

because they laugh and giggle.
This fishing is a test.

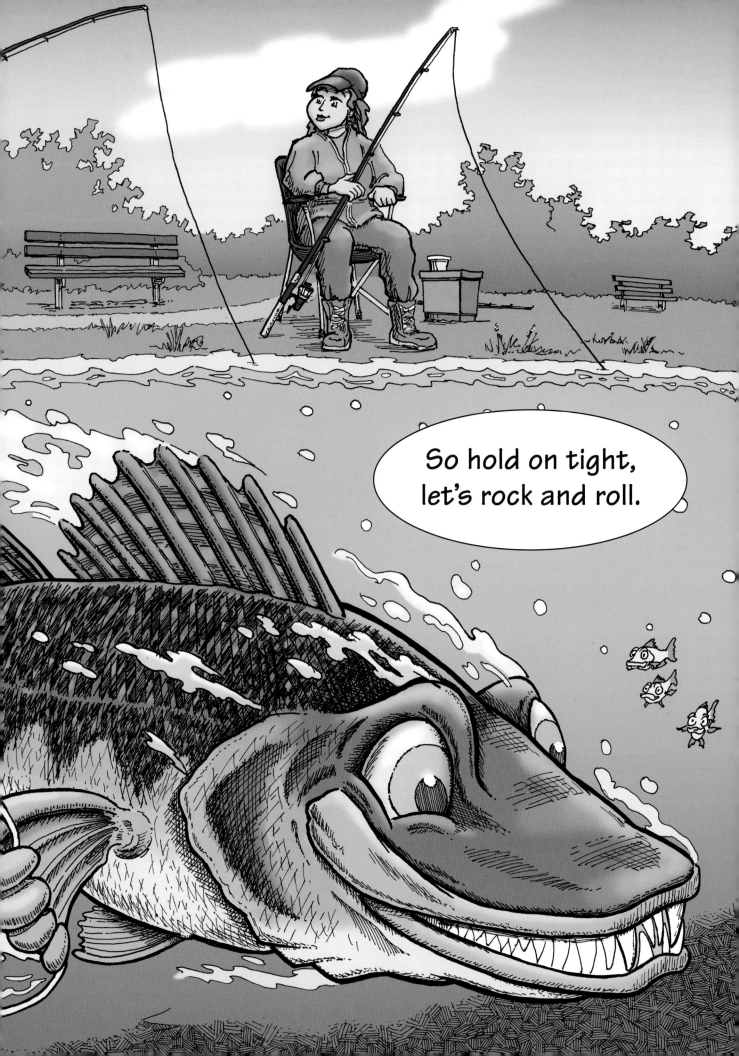

Bob Allen is a Wisconsin author of kids picture books. He features the outdoors and environment as a place to explore and enjoy while maintaining them as a heritage. His focus is on family and fun. "Walter the Wily Walleye" is the story of a fish that invites and challenges a child to try and catch him. Born in Oshkosh, Wisconsin, Bob lives with wife Ann in Brookfield, Wisconsin.

Scott Alberts loves to bring characters to life through illustration. Drawing from nature and the outdoors, he enjoys depicting even the most fanciful of subjects in highly detailed "realistic" style. Based in Northeast Wisconsin, Scott works with authors and other entrepreneurs to bring their ideas to life. Learn more about him at www.scottalberts.com.